CONTENTS

TRADEMARK, COPYRIGHT, OR PATENT

What is a trademark or service mark?

- A trademark is generally a word, phrase, symbol, or design, or a combination thereof, that identifies and distinguishes the source of the goods of one party from those of others.

- A service mark is the same as a trademark, except that it identifies and distinguishes the source of a service rather than goods. Throughout this booklet, the terms "trademark" and "mark" refer to both trademarks and service marks.

Do trademarks, copyrights, and patents protect the same things?

No. Trademarks, copyrights, and patents protect different types of intellectual property. A trademark typically protects brand names and logos used on goods and services. A copyright protects an original artistic or literary work. A patent protects an invention. For example, if you invent a new kind of vacuum cleaner, you would apply for a patent to protect the invention itself. You would apply to register a trademark to protect the brand name of the vacuum cleaner. And you might register a copyright for the TV commercial that you use to market the product.

For copyright information, go to www.copyright.gov. For patent information, go to www.uspto.gov/patents.

To help evaluate your overall awareness of intellectual property knowledge and to provide access to additional educational materials based on the assessment results, please use the Intellectual Property Awareness Assessment tool, available at http://www.uspto.gov/inventors/assessment/.

How do domain names, business name registrations, and trademarks differ?

A domain name is part of a web address that links to the internet protocol address (IP address) of a particular website. For example, in the web address "www.uspto.gov," the domain name is "uspto.gov." You register your domain name with an accredited domain name registrar, not through the USPTO. A domain name and a trademark differ. A trademark identifies goods or services as being from a particular source. Use of a domain name only as part of a web address does not qualify as source-indicating trademark use, though other prominent use apart from the web address may qualify as trademark use. Registration of a domain name with a domain name registrar does not give you any trademark rights. For example, even if you register a certain domain name with a domain name registrar, you could later be required to surrender it if it infringes someone else's trademark rights.

Similarly, use of a business name does not necessarily qualify as trademark use, though other use of a business name as the source of goods or services may qualify it as both a business name and a trademark. Many states and local jurisdictions register business names, either as part of obtaining a certificate to do business or as an assumed name filing. For example, in a state where you will be doing business, you might file documents (typically with a state corporation commission or state division of corporations) to form a business entity, such as a corporation or limited liability company. You would select a name for your entity, for example, XYZ, Inc. If no other company has already applied for that exact name in that state and you comply with all other requirements, the state likely would issue you a certificate and authorize you to do business under that name. However, a state's authorization to form a business with a particular name does not also give you trademark rights and other parties could later try to prevent your use of the business name if they believe a likelihood of confusion exists with their trademarks.

CONSIDERATIONS FOR FEDERAL REGISTRATION WHEN SELECTING A MARK

Once you determine that the type of protection you need is, in fact, trademark protection, then selecting a mark is the very first step in the overall application/registration process. This must be done with thought and care, because not every mark is registrable with the USPTO. Nor is every mark legally protectable, that is, some marks may not be capable of serving as the basis for a legal claim by the owner seeking to stop others from using a similar mark on related goods or services. Businesses and individuals new to trademarks and the application/registration process often choose a mark for their product or service that may be difficult or even impossible to register and/or protect for various reasons. Before filing a trademark/service mark application, you should consider (1) whether the mark you want to register *is* registrable, and (2) how difficult it will be to protect your mark based on the strength of the mark selected. Note in this regard that the USPTO only registers marks. You, as the mark owner, are solely responsible for enforcement.

Below are some factors to consider when choosing a mark. While the USPTO can provide the following general guidance, the agency does not advise you in advance of your filing an application whether your specific mark is registrable.

Likelihood of Confusion with Other Marks

The USPTO examines every application for compliance with federal law and rules. The most common reason to refuse registration is a "likelihood of confusion" between the mark of the applicant and a mark already registered or in a prior-filed pending application owned by another party. The USPTO determines that a likelihood of confusion exists when (1) the marks are similar, and (2) the goods and/or services of the parties are related such that consumers would mistakenly believe they come from the same source. Each application is decided on its own facts and no simple mechanical test is used to determine whether a likelihood of confusion exists. Therefore, before filing your non-refundable application, it is very important for you to determine whether your proposed mark is likely to cause confusion with another mark. This determination can be made only after doing a thorough trademark search, as discussed below.

Example of a likelihood of confusion:

T.MARKEY for "shoes" and TEE MARQEE for "shirts." The marks are similar because they sound identical; and although the goods differ, they are considered related for the purposes of a likelihood of confusion analysis.

Strong v. Weak Marks

In addition to selecting a mark that is not likely to be confused with any pre-existing marks, it is in your best interest to select a mark that is considered "strong" in a legal or trademark sense, i.e., a mark that will most easily allow you to prevent third-party use of your mark. Some marks are easier to protect than others and these are considered "strong" marks.

On the other hand, if a mark is "weak," it most likely is descriptive and others are already using it to describe their goods or services, making it difficult and costly to try to police and protect. Weak marks should be avoided; they simply do not have the same legal protections of a stronger and more distinctive mark.

Generally, marks fall into one of four categories: fanciful or arbitrary, suggestive, descriptive, or generic. The category your mark falls into will significantly impact both its registrability and your ability to enforce your rights in the mark.

The strongest and most easily protectable types of marks are fanciful marks and arbitrary marks, because they are inherently distinctive. Fanciful marks are invented words with no dictionary or other known meaning. Arbitrary marks are actual words with a known meaning that have no association/relationship with the goods protected. Fanciful and arbitrary marks are registrable and, indeed, are more likely to get registered than are descriptive marks. Moreover, because these types of marks are creative and unusual, it is less likely that others are using them.

> Examples of fanciful and arbitrary marks:
>
> Fanciful: BELMICO for "insurance services"
>
> Arbitrary: BANANA for "tires"

Suggestive marks suggest, but do not describe, qualities or a connection to the goods or services. Suggestive marks are registrable and are also considered "strong" marks. If you do not choose a fanciful or arbitrary mark, a suggestive mark is your next best option.

> Examples of suggestive marks:
>
> QUICK N' NEAT for "pie crust"
>
> GLANCE-A-DAY for "calendars"

Descriptive marks are words or designs (e.g., depiction of a television for "television repair services") that describe the goods and/or services. Such marks are generally considered "weaker" and therefore more difficult to protect than fanciful and arbitrary marks. If the USPTO determines that a mark is "merely descriptive," then it is not registrable or protectable on the Principal Register unless it acquires distinctiveness-- generally through extensive use in commerce over a five-year period or longer. Descriptive marks are considered "weak" until they have acquired distinctiveness.

Applicants often choose (frequently at the suggestion of marketing professionals) descriptive marks for their goods and/or services, believing that such marks reduce the need for expensive consumer education and advertising because consumers can immediately identify the product or service being offered directly from the mark. This approach, while perhaps logical marketing advice, often leads to marks that cannot be easily protected, i.e., to extremely weak trademark rights. That is, a descriptive mark may not be registrable or protectable against later users of identical or similar marks; therefore, adoption of a descriptive mark may end up costing more money in the long term, either due to higher costs to try to police and enforce such a mark, or because it may be legally necessary to stop using the descriptive mark and select a new mark.

Examples of descriptive marks:

CREAMY for "yogurt"

WORLD'S BEST BAGELS for "bagels"

Generic words are the weakest types of "marks" (and cannot even qualify as "marks" in the legal sense) and are never registrable or enforceable against third parties. Because generic words are the common, everyday name for goods and services and everyone has the right to use such terms to refer to their goods and services, they are not protectable. Be aware that if you adopt a generic term to identify your goods or services, you will not be able to prevent others from using it to identify potentially competing products or services. In addition, even a fanciful mark that is very strong can, over time, become generic if the owner fails to police use of its mark properly and take appropriate action. Without proper policing over time, the original owner of a mark could lose any trademark rights it has in the mark.

Examples of generic marks:

Applied-for trademarks that would be considered generic at the time of filing because they are the name of the good or product offered by the service:

BICYCLE for "bicycles" or "retail bicycle stores"

MILK for "a dairy-based beverage"

Trademarks that eventually became generic because of long-term widespread, non-trademark use:

ESCALATOR for "moving staircases," ASPIRIN for "pain relief medication"

Other Potential Grounds for the USPTO to Refuse Registration

The USPTO will also refuse registration of a proposed mark for many other reasons, including but not limited to the mark being: a surname; geographically descriptive of the origin of the goods/services; disparaging or offensive; a foreign term that translates to a descriptive or generic term; an individual's name or likeness; the title of a single book and/or movie; and matter that is used in a purely ornamental manner. While some of these refusals are an absolute bar to registration, others may be overcome by evidence under certain circumstances. For more information about these and other possible refusals, see Chapter 1200 of the *Trademark Manual of Examining Procedure (TMEP)* at http://tess2.uspto.gov/tmdb/tmep/.

Other Factors in Selecting a Mark

You should also consider other important factors when selecting your mark, such as whether the public is likely to be able to remember, pronounce, and spell the selected mark. If you plan to market your goods or services outside the United States under the same mark, consider whether the U.S. mark might have another meaning when translated into a foreign language, particularly if, for example, the translated word could be considered offensive.

TRADEMARK SEARCHING

Why should I do a trademark search?

Conducting a complete search of your mark before filing an application is very important because the results may identify potential problems, such as a likelihood of confusion with a prior registered mark or a mark in a pending application. A search could save you the expense of applying for a mark in which you will likely not receive a registration because another party may already have stronger rights in that mark. Also, the search results may show whether your mark or a part of your mark appears as generic or descriptive wording in other registrations, and thus is weak and/or difficult to protect.

How do I search?

The USPTO offers a free search system known as TESS (Trademark Electronic Search System), available 24-7 through http://www.uspto.gov/trademarks at "TESS search trademarks." The TESS Help Page at http://tess2.uspto.gov/webaka/html/help.htm includes information, with some sample search strategies, on how to search the USPTO's database of registered and prior pending applications to help determine whether any marks therein could prevent registration of your mark due to a likelihood of confusion. The USPTO will not search your mark for you prior to your filing an application. After filing and as part of the examination of your application, the USPTO will conduct a search of your mark and will let you know the results of that search. If the USPTO finds another registered mark or earlier-filed pending mark confusingly similar to yours for related goods/services, it will refuse to register your mark.

Alternatively, you can search the TESS database at a Patent and Trademark Resource Center (PTRC). Information about PTRC locations is available through www.uspto.gov under "Products & Services."

Be aware that any searches you conduct on TESS are limited to the USPTO's database of federal trademark applications and registrations and do not include the marks of other parties who may have trademark rights but no federal registration. In the United States, parties are not required to register their marks to obtain protectable rights. Therefore, you should seriously consider whether to hire a trademark attorney to assist you with a "full" or "comprehensive" trademark search, as discussed below.

PRIVATE TRADEMARK ATTORNEYS AND HOW TO FIND ONE

Do I need a lawyer?

Filing a trademark application at the USPTO starts a legal proceeding that may be complex and will require you to comply with all requirements of the trademark statute and rules. Most applicants hire an attorney who specializes in trademark matters to represent them in the application process and provide legal advice. While a USPTO trademark examining attorney will try to help you through the process even if you do not hire a lawyer, no USPTO attorney may give you legal advice. Once you hire an attorney, the USPTO will only communicate with your attorney about your application.

A private trademark attorney can help you before, during, and after the trademark application process, including helping you police and enforce the trademark registration that may issue from your application. While you are not required to have an attorney, an attorney may save you from future costly legal problems by conducting a comprehensive search of federal registrations, state registrations, and "common law" unregistered trademarks—all done before you file your application. Comprehensive searches are important because other trademark owners may have stronger protected legal rights in trademarks similar to yours even though they are not federally registered. Therefore, those unregistered trademarks will not appear in the USPTO's Trademark Electronic Search System (TESS) database but could still ultimately prevent you from using your mark even if the USPTO registers your mark.

In addition, trademark lawyers can help you navigate the application process to provide optimal protection of your trademark rights, by, for example, accurately identifying and classifying your goods and services, and preparing responses to any refusals to register that an examining attorney may issue. Further, a private attorney can help you understand the scope of your trademarks rights and advise you on the best way to police and enforce those rights, including what to do if other trademark owners allege that you are infringing their mark. Remember, enforcement of trademark rights is your responsibility, not that of the USPTO.

How do I find a trademark attorney?

To locate an attorney, consult your local telephone listings, the Internet, or contact the attorney referral service of a state bar or local bar association (for assistance in that regard, see the American Bar Association's Consumers' Guide to Legal Help, at http://apps.americanbar.org/legalservices/findlegalhelp/home.cfm). The USPTO cannot provide you with legal advice or help you select an attorney.

SHOULD I REGISTER MY MARK?

Is federal registration of my mark required?

No. You can establish rights in a mark based on use of the mark in commerce, without a registration. However, owning a federal trademark registration on the Principal Register provides a number of advantages, including:

- A legal presumption of your ownership of the mark and your exclusive right to use the mark nationwide on or in connection with the goods/services listed in the registration (whereas a state registration only provides rights within the borders of that one state);

- Public notice of your claim of ownership of the mark;

- Listing in the USPTO's online databases;

- The ability to record the U.S. registration with the U.S. Customs and Border Protection Service to prevent importation of infringing foreign goods;

- The right to use the federal registration symbol "®";

- The ability to bring an action concerning the mark in federal court; and

- The use of the U.S. registration as a basis to obtain registration in foreign countries.

When can I use the trademark symbols TM, SM, and ®?

If you claim rights to use a mark, you may use the "TM" (trademark) or "SM" (service mark) designation to alert the public to your claim of ownership of the mark, regardless of whether you have filed an application with the United States Patent and Trademark Office (USPTO). However, you may only use the federal registration symbol "®" after the USPTO actually registers a mark, and not while an application is pending. You may only use the registration symbol with the mark on or in connection with the goods/services listed in the federal trademark registration. However, no specific requirements exist as to the precise use of the "®" symbol as to placement, e.g., whether used in a subscript or superscript manner. Note: Several foreign countries use "®" to indicate that a mark is registered in that country. Use of the symbol by the holder of a foreign registration may be proper.

WHAT THE USPTO DOES AND DOES NOT DO

What does the USPTO do?

The USPTO reviews trademark applications and determines whether the applied-for mark meets the requirements for federal registration. USPTO employees will answer general questions about the application process at no charge. Contact the Trademark Assistance Center (TAC) at TrademarkAssistanceCenter@uspto.gov or 1-800-786-9199. Note: The USPTO cannot provide any sort of information in the nature of "legal advice." For legal advice, please consider contacting an attorney who specializes in intellectual property.

What does the USPTO not do?

The USPTO does not:

- Decide whether you have the right to use a mark (which differs from the right to register). No law requires that you federally register your mark in order to acquire rights in the mark;

- Enforce your rights in the mark or bring legal action against a potential infringer.

- Conduct trademark searches for the public;

- Comment on the validity of registered marks;

- Assist you with policing your mark against infringers;

- Assist you with recordation of your mark with U.S. Customs and Border Protection;

- Answer questions prior to filing on whether a particular mark or type of mark is eligible for trademark registration; or

- Offer legal advice or opinions about common law trademark rights, state registrations, or trademark infringement claims.

HOW TO FILE A TRADEMARK APPLICATION

Is there a form for filing my application?

Yes. You can file your application directly over the Internet using the Trademark Electronic Application System (TEAS) at http://www.uspto.gov/teas. Two options are available: regular TEAS and TEAS Plus. Both options allow you to pay by credit card, electronic funds transfer, or through an existing USPTO deposit account. Electronic filing has many advantages over filing on paper, including:

- On-line help. Hyperlinks provide help sections for each of the application fields. Help is also available from TEAS@uspto.gov and from the Trademark Assistance Center (TAC) (TrademarkAssistanceCenter@uspto.gov or 1-800-786-9199).

- Validation function. TEAS checks information to help avoid the omission of important information.

- Immediate reply. The USPTO immediately issues an initial filing receipt via e-mail containing the assigned application serial number and a summary of the submission.

- 24-hour availability. TEAS is available 24 hours a day, 7 days a week (except 2 a.m. to 6 a.m.

Sundays when you cannot pay by credit card, although you can create forms and save them for later filing). You can receive a filing date until midnight Eastern Standard Time on any date.

- Lower filing fees. The filing fee for using TEAS is lower than the fee for filing on paper. If you use the TEAS Plus form, the fee is even lower than the regular TEAS application.

- More accurate filing receipts. Most of your information is transferred directly from what you enter into the database and is generally not re-entered by hand at the USPTO.

If you do not have Internet access, you can access TEAS at any Patent and Trademark Resource Center (PTRC) throughout the United States (see http://www.uspto.gov/products/library/ptdl/locations/index.jsp). Many public libraries also provide Internet access.

What is the difference between the regular TEAS and the TEAS Plus application options?

The filing fee for a regular TEAS application is $325 per class of goods/services. The TEAS Plus application has a lower filing fee of $275 per class of goods/services, and you must meet certain additional requirements. For example, you must be able to select an entry or entries from the USPTO's *Acceptable Identification of Goods and Services Manual (ID Manual)* (available at http://tess2.uspto.gov/netahtml/tidm.html) that accurately describe your goods/services. Additionally, you must file communications regarding the application through TEAS, and receive communications concerning the application by e-mail. If you fail to meet the TEAS Plus requirements, the USPTO will require that you pay an additional fee of $50 per class.

Can I file other than by the Internet?

Yes. We recommend using TEAS, but you may file a paper application at a higher cost of $375 per class of goods/services. To obtain a printed form, call the USPTO's automated telephone line at 1-800-786-9199. Our mailing address is Commissioner for Trademarks, P.O. Box 1451, Alexandria, VA 22313-1451. You may **not** submit an application by facsimile.

Note: Please confirm that all fees referenced above are current, either through the Trademark Fee Information page at http://www.uspto.gov/trademarks/tm_fee_info.jsp or by calling the Trademark Assistance Center (TAC) at 1-800-786-9199.

WHAT A FILING DATE IS AND HOW IT IS DETERMINED

All applications are assigned a filing date. If you transmit your application over the Internet, the filing date is the date the transmission reaches the USPTO server, in Eastern Standard Time. If you file on paper, the filing date of an application is the date the USPTO receives the application. The USPTO relies on a filing date to assess priority among applications; i.e., the USPTO reviews applications in the order received. The filing date is important because it generally gives your application priority over applications with a later filing date. So, if an application filed after yours is likely to cause confusion with yours, that application will be blocked, or, technically, suspended, until your application either registers or goes abandoned.

The priority created by a filing date is not absolute. You might have very strong rights based on long use of your mark, for example, even if this is the first time filing for a federal registration. So, if you are second in line but you have stronger rights than the applicant in front of you, you may be able to intervene with an opposition proceeding and prevent that application from registering. So while examination will not take place out of order, the second in line does have an opportunity to assert superior rights at the proper time in the overall registration process.

Receiving a filing date does not mean that your mark will be registered. To obtain a registration, you must comply with all application requirements and overcome any refusal(s) issued by the USPTO during examination.

INFORMATION TO INCLUDE IN THE APPLICATION

- OWNER OF THE MARK ("APPLICANT")
- NAME AND ADDRESS FOR CORRESPONDENCE
- DEPICTION OF THE MARK ("THE DRAWING")
- GOODS/SERVICES
- APPLICATION FILING FEE
- BASIS FOR FILING
- SPECIMEN FOR USE-BASED APPLICATIONS
- SIGNATURE

OWNER OF THE MARK (APPLICANT)

The application must be filed in the name of the owner of the mark. The owner of the mark is the person or entity who controls the nature and quality of the goods/services identified by the mark. The owner is not necessarily the name of the person filling out the form. The owner may be an individual, corporation, partnership, LLC, or other type of legal entity.

Must I be a U.S. citizen to apply?

No. You are not required to be a U.S. citizen to apply for and obtain a federal registration.

NAME AND ADDRESS FOR CORRESPONDENCE

The applicant's name and street address is required for the USPTO to send communications concerning the application. The applicant is strongly encouraged to provide an e-mail address and authorize the USPTO to correspond electronically, to allow the USPTO to e-mail notices regarding the application. Applicants who file using the TEAS Plus form must authorize e-mail communication. Note: The USPTO is not responsible for any e-mail not received due to the applicant's security or anti-spam software, or any problems within the applicant's e-mail system. You can view all sent actions and notices on-line, from Trademark Status and Document Retrieval (http://tsdr.uspto.gov/).

Applicants who reside outside the United States may include the name and address of a domestic representative on their application. A domestic representative is a person residing in the U.S. upon whom notices or process may be served for proceedings affecting the mark.

Changes of Address: You must keep your mailing address and/or e-mail address up to date with the USPTO. Changes of address should be filed using the Change of Correspondence Address form on TEAS at http://www.uspto.gov/teas. If you send a change of address on paper, please include the applicant's name, the mark, and the application serial number and mail to: Commissioner for Trademarks, P.O. Box 1451, Alexandria, VA 22313-1451.

Warning for Privacy Concerns

Except for payment information, all data you submit to the USPTO, including your street address, e-mail address, and telephone number, will become part of a public record and will be viewable through the Internet on the USPTO's website, as well as other websites that index USPTO data, such as Google®.com. Some applicants use a Post Office box number to avoid disclosure of a physical address. While providing your telephone number will help the USPTO communicate with you, it is not required; therefore, if you do not wish your telephone number to become public, please do not provide it.

Non-USPTO Communications about Your Trademark

Solicitations: Third-party websites and Internet search engines may use and post the information you provide to the USPTO and companies not associated with the USPTO may use the information to mail or e-mail you solicitations concerning your trademark. These companies may use names that resemble the USPTO name, including, for example, the terms "United States" or "U.S," and their solicitations often mimic the look of official government documents rather than appearing like a typical commercial or legal solicitation by emphasizing official government data like the USPTO application serial number, the registration number, the International Class(es), filing dates, and other information that is publicly available from USPTO records. Many refer to other government agencies and sections of the U.S. Code. Most require "fees" to be paid.

So, be sure to read trademark-related communications carefully before making a decision about whether to respond. All official correspondence will be from the "United States Patent and Trademark Office" in Alexandria, VA, and if by e-mail, specifically from the domain "@uspto.gov."

Letters claiming trademark infringement: If another trademark owner believes that you do not have the right to use your trademark, you may receive a letter (a "cease-and-desist" letter) that (1) requests that you stop using your mark because of what the letter will allege is unlawful or infringing use, and (2) states that you could face possible legal action if you do not stop using your mark. Because of the legal implication regarding the rights in your mark and the threat of possible legal action against you, if an attorney does not already represent you, you are strongly encouraged to hire one. Please see the "How do I find a trademark attorney" section on page 6.

DEPICTION OF THE MARK ("THE DRAWING")

Every application must include a clear image of one mark ("the drawing"). The USPTO uses the drawing to upload the mark into the USPTO search database and to print the mark in the Official Gazette and on the registration certificate. If you have variations on the mark that you wish to register, each requires its own separate application and fee.

There are two types of drawings: "standard character" and "special form."

What is a "standard character" drawing?

A standard character drawing is commonly submitted when the mark you wish to register consists solely of words, letters, or numbers. A standard character mark protects the wording itself, without limiting the mark to a specific font, style, size, or color and therefore gives you broader protection than a special form drawing.

A standard character drawing must have the following characteristics:

- No design element;
- No stylization of lettering and/or numbers;
- Any letters and words in Latin characters;
- Any numbers in Roman or Arabic numerals;
- Only common punctuation or diacritical marks.

NOTE: The USPTO has created a standard character set that lists letters, numerals, punctuation marks, and diacritical marks that may be used in a standard character drawing. The set is available on the USPTO's website at http://teas.uspto.gov/standardCharacterSet.html.

How do I file a standard character drawing?

When you file electronically, TEAS generates a standard character drawing for you, based on the information you enter on the form under "enter the mark here."

When you file on paper, you must use standard letter-size paper and include these elements at the top of the "drawing page" as part of your application: applicant's name; correspondence address; and the following statement: "The mark is presented in standard character format without claim to any particular font style, size or color." The representation of the mark must appear in the middle of the page.

What is a "special form" drawing?

If your mark includes a design or logo, alone or with wording, or if the particular style of lettering or particular color(s) is important, you must select the "special form" drawing format. If you are seeking registration of a word(s) combined with a design element, the drawing must depict both the word(s) and the design element combined as one image.

How do I file a "special form" drawing?

When you file electronically, you must upload an image of your mark into the TEAS form. The mark image must be in .jpg format and should have minimal white space surrounding the design of the mark. Mark images should not include the trademark, service mark or registration symbols (TM, SM, ®). Unless a color image is being submitted for a mark wherein color is claimed as a feature of the mark, the mark image should be black and white.

When you file on paper, you must use standard letter-size paper and include the applicant's name and correspondence address at the top of the drawing page as part of your application. The mark must appear in the middle of the page, and consist of the entire mark, i.e., word(s) and design, where appropriate.

The following is an example of a proper special form drawing page for an application filed on paper for the mark T.MARKEY and the design of the T.MARKEY character:

Applicant's Name: Jefferson Partners, Inc.

Correspondence Address: 100 Main Street, Any Town, MO 12345

Should I submit a black-and-white drawing or a color drawing?

Generally, you may submit a black-and-white drawing even if you use your mark in color, because a black-and-white drawing covers use of your mark in any color. However, if it is important that your customers associate specific colors in your mark with your product, you may wish to limit your mark and claim those colors as part of your mark. If you do submit a color claim, then you must also submit a color drawing of your mark that matches the colors you are claiming.

What are the requirements if I submit a color drawing?

You must submit the following: (1) a "color claim" naming the color(s) and stating that the color(s) is a feature of the mark, and (2) a separate statement describing the mark and stating where the color(s) appears in the mark.

GOODS/SERVICES

What is the difference between goods and services?

Goods are products, such as bicycles or candles. Services are activities performed for the benefit of someone else, such as bicycle rental services or catering.

The difference between goods and services may be confusing. Are your customers paying for a product or paying you to perform a specific activity? If your customer is paying you for a product, such as a candle or bicycle, then you have goods. However, if your customer is paying you to perform an activity, such as catering or bicycle rental, then you have services. You may list both goods and services in an application.

You must list the specific goods/services for which you want to register your mark. If you are filing based upon "use in commerce," you must be using the mark in commerce on all the goods/services listed. If you are filing based upon a "bona fide intent to use the mark," you must have a good faith or bona fide intent to use the mark on all the goods/services listed.

You should check the USPTO's *Acceptable Identification of Goods and Services Manual (ID Manual)* at http://tess2.uspto.gov/netahtml/tidm.html, which contains a listing of acceptable identifications of goods and services. Any entry you choose must accurately describe your goods/services. A failure to correctly list the goods/services with which you use the mark, or intend to use the mark, may prevent you from registering your mark. You will not be given a refund of any fees paid.

If the *ID Manual* does not contain an accurate listing for your goods/services, do not merely select an entry that seems "close." Instead, you must create your own identification, describing your goods/services using clear, concise terms that the general public easily understands. If you list vague terms, such as "miscellaneous services" or "company name," your application will be considered void and you must file a new application.

If using the TEAS PLUS form, you must choose your goods/services from the *ID Manual*. Therefore, you should check the *ID Manual* prior to filling out the form. If no *ID Manual* entry accurately identifies your goods/services, you may **not** use the TEAS PLUS form. However, you *may* use the regular TEAS form.

May I change the goods/services after filing my application?

You may clarify or limit the goods/services but you may not expand or broaden the goods/services. For example, if you filed for "shirts," you may limit the goods to specific types of shirts such as "t-shirts and sweatshirts." However, you may not change the goods to "pants." Likewise, if you file for "jewelry," you may change the goods to specific types of jewelry such as "jewelry, namely, earrings." However, you may not change the goods to a service such as "jewelry stores."

APPLICATION FILING FEE

Application filing fees are based on the type of application form used (paper, regular TEAS, or TEAS Plus) and the number of International Classes of Goods or Services in the application. Paper applications have the highest filing fee and TEAS Plus applications have the lowest filing fee. For current fees, see the Trademark Fee Information page at http://www.uspto.gov/trademarks/tm_fee_info.jsp or contact the Trademark Assistance Center (TAC) (TrademarkAssistanceCenter@uspto.gov or 1-800-786-9199).

Goods and services are sorted into categories called "International Classes." Each International Class requires a separate filing fee. For a listing of the International Classes, see the International Schedule of Classes of Goods and Services, at http://www.uspto.gov/trademarks/notices/international.jsp. While you can use the schedule to determine the total number of classes that require a fee (each class of goods and services requires a separate fee), it is not appropriate for determining actual identifications of goods and/or services to be listed in your application, since general class headings are not acceptable for filing purposes. Instead, use the USPTO's *Acceptable Identification of Goods and Services Manual (ID Manual)*, at http://tess2.uspto.gov/netahtml/tidm.html.

The TEAS and TEAS Plus forms accept payment by credit card and electronic funds transfer or through an existing USPTO deposit account. If you are filing on paper, you can download the form for authorizing credit-card charges from the USPTO website at http://www.uspto.gov/forms/2038-fill.pdf or pay by a check or money order made payable to "Director of the USPTO."

Filing fees are **not** refundable. If your application meets the filing requirements but is later refused on legal grounds, the application filing fee will not be refunded.

BASIS FOR FILING

The application must specify your "basis" for filing. Most U.S. applicants base their application on either their current use of the mark in commerce or their intent to use the mark in commerce in the future.

What is the difference between a "use-in-commerce" application and an "intent-to-use" application?

Under either basis, prior to registration you must demonstrate that you have used the mark in commerce in connection with all the goods/services listed in your application by submitting an acceptable specimen. The basic difference between these two filing bases is whether you have started to use the mark on all the goods/services. If you have already used your mark in commerce in connection with all the goods/services listed in your application, you may file under the "use-in-commerce" basis. If you have not yet used your mark, but intend to use it in the future, you must file under the "intent-to-use" basis. An "intent-to-use" basis requires filing an additional form and fee that are unnecessary if you file under "use in commerce." For information on the additional form, see the "HOW DO I ESTABLISH USE OF THE MARK IF I FILED AN INTENT-TO-USE APPLICATION?" section on page 21. It is also possible to file an application wherein some of the goods/services are in use and others are intent to use, but the application must clearly identify this.

What is a "use-in-commerce" basis?

For applications filed under the use-in-commerce basis, you must be using the mark in the sale or transport of goods or the rendering of services in "interstate" commerce between more than one state or U.S. territory, or in commerce between the U.S. and another country. For goods, the mark must appear on the goods (e.g., tags or labels), the container for the goods, or displays associated with the goods. For services, the mark must be used in the sale or advertising of the services.

How do I establish my "use-in-commerce" basis?

- Provide the date of first use of the mark anywhere and the date of first use of the mark in commerce.

- Submit a specimen (example) showing how you use the mark in commerce. See the "SPECIMEN FOR USE-BASED APPLICATIONS" section on page 17.

What is the difference between the "date of first use anywhere" and the "date of first use in commerce"?

The date of first use anywhere is the date on which the goods were first sold or transported or the services were first provided under the mark even if that use was only local. The date of first use in commerce is the date on which the goods were first sold or transported or the services were first provided under the mark between more than one state or U.S. territory, or in commerce between the U.S. and another country. The date of first use anywhere must be the same as or earlier than the date of first use in commerce.

What is an "intent-to-use" basis?

If you have not yet used the mark but plan to do so in the future, you may file based on a good faith or bona fide intent to use the mark in commerce. A bona fide intent to use the mark is more than an idea and less than market ready. For example, having a business plan, creating sample products, or performing other initial business activities may reflect a bona fide intent to use the mark.

Is there any other possible filing basis?

Yes. Based on international agreements/treaties, an owner may file an application in the U.S. based on a foreign application/registration issued by another country (a "Section 44" application). Also, a foreign owner may file an international application in its home country and request an extension of protection to the U.S. (a "Section 66(a)" application). See *Trademark Manual of Examining Procedure (TMEP)* Chapters 1000 and 1900 for more information.

A USPTO registration is effective only in the U.S., even though the goods/services are assigned an "international" classification number. If after filing a U.S. application you want to protect your mark outside the U.S., you may file an international application or file directly in that country. For more information about protecting your mark under the Madrid Protocol, see http://www.uspto.gov/trademarks/law/madrid/index.jsp.

SPECIMEN FOR USE-BASED APPLICATIONS

What is a "specimen" of use and how does it differ from the "drawing"?

A specimen is a sample of how you actually use the mark in commerce on your goods or with your services. A specimen is not the same as the drawing. The drawing shows only your mark, whereas a specimen shows the mark as your purchasers encounter it in the marketplace (e.g., on the labels or on your website).

What is a proper specimen for use of a mark on goods (products)?

Usually, a specimen for a mark used on goods shows the mark as it appears on the actual goods, or on labeling or packaging for the goods. For example, your specimen may be a tag or label displaying the mark, or a photograph showing the mark on the goods or its packaging. The specimen may not be a "mock-up" of these items but must be a sample of what you actually use or a photograph of the actual packaging. Showing a display of the mark alone is not sufficient; the specimen must show the mark on or in direct connection with the goods.

A specimen that shows the mark being used in a purely ornamental or decorative manner may not be an acceptable specimen. A slogan or a design across the front of a t-shirt or other clothing or a tote bag, for example, would not be acceptable, since it is likely to be perceived as ornamental or decorative rather than a trademark. However, a small word or design, such as a small animal on a shirt pocket, may create the commercial impression of a trademark and be acceptable as a specimen.

Acceptable Specimen   Not Acceptable Specimen

Is my website a proper specimen for goods?

A website is an acceptable specimen if the mark appears near a picture of the goods (or a text description of the goods) and your customers can order the goods from the website. A website that merely advertises the goods is not acceptable. You must provide an actual screenshot of the website; i.e., merely providing the website address is not acceptable.

What is NOT a proper specimen for goods?

Invoices, announcements, order forms, leaflets, brochures, publicity releases, letterhead, and business cards generally are not acceptable specimens for goods.

What is a proper specimen for use of a mark with services?

A specimen for a mark used in connection with services must show the mark used in providing or advertising the services. For example, your specimen may be a photograph of a business sign, a brochure about the services, an advertisement for the services, a website or webpage, a business card, or stationery showing the mark. The specimen must show or contain some reference to the services, that is, it is not just a display of the mark itself.

For example, if the mark sought to be registered is "T.MARKEY" for retail stores featuring men's sportswear, a specimen that only shows the wording "T.MARKEY" and no other matter would not be acceptable, but a specimen that shows the wording "T.MARKEY" on a clothing store sign would be acceptable, as shown on the right.

What is NOT a proper specimen for services?

Printer's proofs for advertisements or news articles about your services are not acceptable because they do not show your use of the mark.

When do I file the specimen?

If your application is based on "use in commerce," you must submit one specimen for each class of goods/services when you file the application.

If your application is based on "intent to use," you must submit one specimen for each class of goods/services when you file the "allegation of use." The allegation of use may be filed prior to publication (Amendment to Allege Use) or after publication (Statement of Use). For more information on the Allegation of Use see the "HOW TO ESTABLISH USE OF THE MARK FOR AN INTENT-TO-USE-APPLICATION" section on page 21.

How do I file the specimen?

When filing electronically, you must attach an image of your specimen in .jpg or .pdf format. To show the context in which the mark is used, the image should include as much of the label or advertisement as possible. In rare instances, your specimen might consist of an audio or video file; please see *TMEP* Section 904.03(f) for further information about submitting these types of specimens.

If you are not able to file by the preferred electronic method and are filing a paper application, Amendment to Allege Use, or Statement of Use, the specimen must be flat and no larger than 8½ by

11 inches (e.g., a label or photograph of the packaging). However, you may submit compact discs, or DVDs, with files in .jpg, .pdf, .wav, .wma, .wmv, .mp3, .mpg, or .avi format.

SIGNATURE

Who may sign the application?

If you own the mark and are applying in your individual capacity and not as a business entity, you may sign the application. If a business entity owns the mark, then the person who may sign the application on behalf of that business is (1) someone with firsthand knowledge of the application contents and authority to act for the owner or (2) someone with legal authority to bind the owner such as a general partner or a corporate officer. If the applicant is represented by an attorney, the attorney may sign the application on behalf of the applicant.

Please note different requirements exist for who may sign other types of documents that applicants must file with the USPTO regarding their application. All documents, including the application, are legal documents; accordingly, the proper person must sign each document for the USPTO to accept it.

How do I sign a TEAS Plus or TEAS application?

In a TEAS application, you enter an electronic signature on the form by typing your signature between two forward slashes. Examples of acceptable signatures for TEAS applications include /john doe/ or /jrd/. It is not permissible for one person to enter another person's signature.

WHAT HAPPENS AFTER FILING AND WHAT TO DO

What must I do after I file the application?

You must diligently monitor the status of your application. This means you must:

- Check the status of your pending application regularly. We recommend that you check your application's status every 3 to 4 months. The assigned examining attorney will review your application approximately 3 months after the filing date. The overall registration process may take up to a year, or even longer, depending on several factors; for example, the basis of filing of the application and the completeness of the application at the time of filing.

- Respond to any issued Office action or notice within the appropriate timeframes, generally within 6 months of the issue date.

- Promptly contact the USPTO and request corrective action if you believe something is incorrect in the file.

How do I check the status?

You may check the status of any pending application through the Trademark Status and Document

Retrieval (TSDR) system, at http://tsdr.uspto.gov/. You must have your serial number available (a serial number is an 8-digit number that generally begins with 76, 77, 79, or 85). If you do not have access to the Internet, you can call the Trademark Assistance Center at 1-800-786-9199 to request a status check.

When you check your application status, make sure that you have received all communications sent to you by the USPTO, made a note of any deadlines, and have taken appropriate action. Also, print a copy of the TSDR status page for your records.

LEGAL AND PROCEDURAL REVIEW OF APPLICATION

Approximately 3 months from the date your application is filed, the application is assigned to an examining attorney to determine whether federal law permits registration. The examining attorney will examine the written application, the drawing, and any specimen, to ensure that they satisfy all of the federal legal requirements. Federal registration of trademarks is governed by the Trademark Act of 1946, 15 U.S.C. §1051 et seq., and the Trademark Rules of Practice, 37 C.F.R. Part 2.

The examining attorney may issue a letter (Office action) explaining any reasons for refusing registration or other requirements. If you receive an Office action, you must submit a response within 6 months of the issue date of the Office action. Your filing fee will **not** be refunded if the application is refused registration.

PUBLICATION FOR OPPOSITION

If no refusals or additional requirements are identified or if all identified issues have been resolved, the examining attorney will approve the mark for publication in the *Official Gazette (OG)*, a weekly online publication. The USPTO will send you a Notice of Publication stating the publication date.

If you have authorized e-mail communication, the USPTO will e-mail you a "Notification of 'Notice of Publication'" approximately 3 weeks before the future publication date in the *OG*. On the actual publication date, you will receive a second e-mail, namely, "*Official Gazette* Publication Confirmation" with a link to the *OG*. If you have not authorized e-mail communication with the USPTO, the USPTO will mail you approximately 3 weeks before publication a paper "Notice of Publication" stating the publication date.

WHAT HAPPENS AFTER PUBLICATION?

After publication in the *OG*, there is a 30-day period in which the public may object to the registration of the mark by filing an opposition. An opposition is similar to a court proceeding, but is held before the Trademark Trial and Appeal Board, a USPTO administrative tribunal. A third party who is considering filing an opposition may first file a request for an extension of time to file the opposition, which could delay further action on your application.

The next step after publication depends on your basis for filing the application:

REGISTRATION CERTIFICATE ISSUES FOR "USE-IN-COMMERCE" APPLICATION

If no opposition or extension of time to oppose is filed or if you successfully overcome an opposition, you do not need to take any action for the application to enter the next stage of the process. Absent any opposition-related filings, the USPTO generally will issue a registration certificate about 11 weeks after publication, if the application is based upon the actual use of the mark in commerce (Section 1(a)) or on a foreign or international registration (Section 44(e) or Section 66(a)).

NOTICE OF ALLOWANCE (NOA) ISSUES FOR "INTENT-TO-USE" APPLICATION

If no opposition or extension of time to oppose is filed or you successfully overcome an opposition, you do not need to take any action for the application to enter the next stage of the process. Absent any opposition-related filings, the USPTO generally will issue a NOA about 8 weeks after publication.

A NOA indicates that your mark has been allowed, but does not mean that it has registered. As the next step to registration, within 6 months of the issue date of the NOA you must:

- Submit a "Statement of Use" if you filed based on intent to use (Section 1(b)) and are now using the mark in commerce;

- Begin using the mark in commerce and then submit a "Statement of Use;" or

- Submit a six-month "Request for an Extension of Time to File a Statement of Use" if you need additional time to begin using the mark in commerce.

Forms for filing both the Statement of Use and Extension of Time are at http://www.uspto.gov/teas.

HOW TO ESTABLISH USE OF THE MARK FOR AN "INTENT-TO-USE" APPLICATION

Notice of Allowance (NOA) Has Already Issued

If a NOA has already issued, you establish use by filing a Statement of Use (SOU) form that contains a sworn statement that you are now using the mark in commerce on all the goods/services. If you wish to file an SOU before the mark is in use in commerce on all listed goods/services, you must delete or divide out the goods/services for which the mark is not in use. For more on division of an application, please see *TMEP* §1110 et seq.

The SOU must also include:

- A filing fee of $100 per class of goods/services;

- The date of first use of the mark anywhere and the date of first use of the mark in commerce; and

- One specimen (or example) showing how you use the mark in commerce for each class of goods/services.

Once the USPTO issues the NOA, you have 6 months to file the SOU. The 6-month period runs from the issue date shown on the NOA, not the date you receive it. If you have not used the mark in commerce, you must file a Request for an Extension of Time to File a Statement of Use (Extension Request) before the end of the 6-month period, or the application will be declared abandoned, meaning that the application process has ended and your mark will not register. You may request 5 additional extensions for up to a total of 36 months from the NOA issue date, with a statement of your ongoing efforts to make use of the mark in commerce. A filing fee of $150 per class of goods/services must accompany each Extension Request. The form for filing the Extension Request is at http://www.uspto.gov/teas. The date of the grant or denial of an Extension Request does not affect the deadline for filing the SOU or next Extension Request. The deadline is always calculated from the issue date of the NOA.

Notice of Allowance (NOA) Has Not Yet Issued

If the NOA has not yet issued and the application has not yet been approved for publication, you may file an Amendment to Allege Use, which includes the same information as the SOU (see above). You may not file the Amendment to Allege Use during the "blackout period" after approval of the mark for publication and before issuance of the NOA. In that situation, you must wait until after the blackout period to file your SOU.

MAINTAINING A FEDERAL TRADEMARK REGISTRATION

To maintain your trademark registration, you must file your first maintenance document between the 5th and 6th year after the registration date and other maintenance documents thereafter. Your registration certificate contains important information on maintaining your federal registration. The USPTO does not currently send reminder notices when the documents are due. If the documents are not timely filed, your registration will be cancelled and cannot be revived or reinstated, making the filing of a brand new application to begin the overall process again necessary. Forms for filing the maintenance documents are at http://www.uspto.gov/teas.

Throughout the life of the registration, you must police and enforce your rights. While the USPTO will prevent another pending application for a similar mark used on related goods or in connection with related services from proceeding to registration based on a finding of likelihood of confusion, the USPTO will not engage in any separate policing or enforcement activities.

Rights in a federally registered trademark can last indefinitely if you continue to use the mark and file all necessary maintenance documents with the required fee(s) at the appropriate times, as identified below. The necessary documents for maintaining a trademark registration are:

- Declaration of Continued Use or Excusable Nonuse under Section 8 (§8 declaration); and

- Combined Declaration of Continued Use and Application for Renewal under Sections 8 and 9 (combined §§8 and 9).

A §8 declaration is due before the end of the 6-year period after the registration date or within the 6-month grace period thereafter. Failure to file this declaration will result in the cancellation of the registration.

A combined §§8 and 9 must be filed before the end of every 10-year period after the registration date or within the 6-month grace period thereafter. Failure to make these required filings will result in cancellation and/or expiration of the registration.

For further information, including information regarding the special requirements that apply to Madrid Protocol registrations, use the Popular Link "Maintain or Renew Registrations" on the left side of the Trademarks Home page (http://uspto.gov/trademarks/index.jsp) or contact the Trademark Assistance Center (TAC) (TrademarkAssistanceCenter@uspto.gov or 1-800-786-9199).

FEES FOR FILING TRADEMARK-RELATED DOCUMENTS

Current fees for all trademark filings are available via the Trademark Fee Information page at http://www.uspto.gov/trademarks/tm_fee_info.jsp or can be obtained from Trademark Assistance Center (TAC) (TrademarkAssistanceCenter@uspto.gov or 1-800-786-9199).

For the following documents, fees are based on the total number of International Classes that the USPTO assigns to your goods/services. For a listing of the International Classes, see the "International Schedule of Classes of Goods and Services," at http://www.uspto.gov/trademarks/notices/international.jsp.

Initial Application Forms

- TEAS Plus application - $275 per international class

- TEAS application - $325 per international class

- Paper application - $375 per international class

Intent-to-Use Forms

- Amendment to Allege Use (AAU) - $100 per international class

- Statement of Use (SOU) - $100 per international class

- Request for Extension of Time to file SOU- $150 per international class

Post-Registration Maintenance Fees

- Declaration of Continued Use or Excusable Nonuse under Section 8 (§8 declaration) - $100 per international class

- Combined Declaration of Continued Use and Application for Renewal under Sections 8 and 9 (combined §§8 and 9) - $500 per international class

FOR MORE INFORMATION

- **USPTO website at www.uspto.gov/trademarks, First-Time Filers, Start Here, Trademark Basics**
  For instructional videos, application processing timelines, frequently asked questions (FAQs), and other useful information.

- **Trademark Assistance Center (TAC) TrademarkAssistanceCenter@uspto.gov or 1-800-786-9199**
  For general trademark information and printed application forms

- **Patent and Trademark Resource Centers**
  Patent and Trademark Resource Centers (PTRCs) are a nationwide network of public, state, and academic libraries that disseminate patent and trademark information and support the diverse intellectual property needs of the public. The PTRCs have trained specialists who may answer specific questions regarding the trademark process, but they do not provide legal advice. More information on PTRCs, including a list of the PTRC(s) in your state, is available at www.uspto.gov under "Products & Services."